A PRIMER ON PARALLEL LIVES

OTHER BOOKS BY DAN GERBER

Poetry

Trying to Catch the Horses (Michigan State University Press, 1999)
A Last Bridge Home: New and Selected Poems (Clark City Press, 1992)
Snow on the Backs of Animals (Winn Books, 1986)
The Chinese Poems (Sumac Press, 1978)
Departure (Sumac Press, 1973)
The Revenant (Sumac Press, 1971)

Novels

A Voice from the River (Clark City Press, 1990; Michigan State University Press, 2005)
Out of Control (Prentice Hall, 1974; Warner Paperback Library, 1975)
American Atlas (Prentice Hall, 1973; Michigan State University Press, 2003)

Short Stories

Grass Fires (Winn Books, 1987; Clark City Press, 1989, 1999; Michigan State University Press, 2003)

Nonfiction

A Second Life: A Collected Nonfiction (Michigan State University Press, 2001)
Indy: The World's Fastest Carnival Ride (Prentice Hall, 1977)

A Primer on Parallel Lives

DAN GERBER

For Diana Chase,
friend, Neighbor and fellow
rustler.
    With my best wishes,
      Dan Gerber
      Santa Ynez
      April 2008

Copper Canyon Press

Cover art: Winslow Homer, *Fox Hunt,* 1893. Oil on canvas, 38" × 68½". Courtesy of the Pennsylvania Academy of the Fine Arts, Philadelphia, and the Joseph E. Temple Fund.

Copper Canyon Press is in residence at Fort Worden State Park in Port Townsend, Washington, under the auspices of Centrum Foundation. Centrum is a gathering place for artists and creative thinkers from around the world, students of all ages and backgrounds, and audiences seeking extraordinary cultural enrichment.

LIBRARY OF CONGRESS CATALOGING-IN-PUBLICATION DATA

Gerber, Dan, 1940–
A Primer on parallel lives / Dan Gerber.
   p. cm.
ISBN-13: 978-1-55659-253-9 (pbk.: alk. paper)
1. Title.
PS3557.E66P75 2007
811'.54 — dc22

2006031656

9 8 7 6 5 4 3 2   FIRST PRINTING

COPPER CANYON PRESS
Post Office Box 271
Port Townsend, Washington 98368

www.coppercanyonpress.org

ACKNOWLEDGMENTS

Publications in which some of these poems have previously appeared:

American Life in Poetry (The Poetry Foundation), *Art Life, The Café Review, Chicago Atheneum Anthology, Fairfield Review, Growing a Masterpiece* (Fred Meijer Sculpture Garden publication), *New Letters, Oyster Boy Review, Parting Gifts, Pegasus, Red Cedar Review, Saying What Needs to Be Said: Central Coast Poets* (Solo Press), *Snowy Egret, Solo,* and *Tangram Press* broadsides. "The Man Jumping" and "Sail Baby Sail" appeared originally in *A Last Bridge Home* (Clark City Press, 1992).

For Deb

Every sudden heightening of intensity brought you into a god's sphere of influence. And, within that sphere, the god in question would fight against or ally himself with other gods on a second stage alive with presences. From that moment on, every event, every encounter occurred in parallel in two places. To tell a story meant to weave those two series of parallel events together, to make both worlds visible.

ROBERTO CALASSO

Contents

A PRIMER ON PARALLEL LIVES

ONE

I am not I.

I am this one

walking beside me...

J.R. JIMÉNEZ

In Praise of Umberto Tapia

I cup my hands around the last bright speck
and blow gently to keep it alive, an ember
of oak log, pared from a tree
Umberto Tapia rescued with his artful pruning,
from stifling mistletoe and Spanish moss,
and the unleavened abundance that
drags it down, a life like my own
from which too little has been let go.

Now I see this coal
as a fallen star,
one bright thing in a field of night,
curious about the darkness
and the world kneeling down to it,
using its breath to keep it glowing.

Tracking the Moment

The place where I stopped last night is far away;
and tomorrow, tonight will be last night.

YANG WAN-LI (1127–1206)

A million stars
made by sun and wind
on the water of a pond
where I stood once
and gazed from a house no longer standing
with a woman no longer living,
both so clear to me now,
remembering light on the waves of Lake Michigan
where my seven-year-old feet
made tracks in the sand
toward water
where all tracks dissolve
till the stars return with sunlight and memory
as the breeze rises.

I

Weather comes up easily here in the mountains.
This day, darkening before noon
with ominous clouds, and then,
as if to mock them,
a shaft of sun comes through.

Setting off up the valley with no destination
other than this place from which I began,
I suppose it's finally the story of our lives,
an innocence nothing can equal.

Turning north to the edge of a hayfield,
skirting its border of scrub oak and pine—
leaving the mysterious forest unentered—
a dense sandwich of years, my shoes kick up
echoes and dust.

*

Aimless motorcycle rides
through canyons and vineyards
with roses at the ends of the vine rows,
great rolling plains and dark mountain passes,
steeped in wild rosemary,
with hayfields ready for cutting, or just cut,
old cow dung and green cow dung,
a whiff of petroleum and yeast,
slowing through a block-long Main Street,
passing an abandoned gas station and a bar
airing out on Sunday morning, smells
almost forgotten, the dark, freshly turned soil,
where two workmen are digging
at the edge of the road,
copper smell of a crushed cat
in the grass on the shoulder,
and the smell of the virga,
a silhouette of rain,
a scent of pure promise,
like the promise of our breath,

falling, yet never
coming to the ground.

2

God, is that you
tapping on my shutters this morning,
your redheaded herald,
the flicker,
opening small cracks
in the roof I've spent so much to maintain,
breaching the insulation of the phone lines
so the rains, now come,
make them bristle and pop,
your language my arrogance won't let me decipher?

Fog settles on my hair and glasses
while I wait for traces of the view to reemerge.
How little we see even on the best days,
a few details,
broken grass stalks along the deer trail,
oaks swept eastward from the wind off the sea,
a few fragments of bone and feathers,
the intrigue of a life interrupted,
now that the hills have wrapped themselves in clouds.

Stars go on watching through this long afternoon
while I breathe in the sky and am still not filled.
The sun, a galaxy of blood through my eyelids;
wind now a river of smoke
through the long grass over the hills.

        3

I am always returning to the edge of water,
lapping at the loam of a bank under pine needles,
and slapping at the bellies of dock planks.
Or I'm looking into one of those still, black ponds,
which seems to me like a pupil of the planet,
through which it watches the other stars
and finally our own silent faces,
gazing down to its ever-intensified heart.

              ◆

Our boatman tells us
he's rowed this passage over three thousand times,
the distance around the Earth's waist,
in this nine-mile stretch of river.

Today an autumn wind
holds us a moment in stasis against the flow
as we squint through the rain toward a glint of sun
a mile downstream.

Three elk—cow, calf, and bull—
trot into the pines as we approach,
only to put a few boughs,
like another language, between us.

❦

And what do the animals really know about our lives?
It seems they look on with unclouded ambition
to simply be more what they are
while we go on longing for their kind of grace.

Every night for three months, the fox
came to my bedroom window
and, in the wildness of her call,
I heard something so certain it stunned my heart
with what I once was, and may
yet be.

4

To stones on the riverbed
the current is a constant breeze,
the wind of the Earth's turning
we can't feel anymore.

I lift my fly through moving air
for the joy of laying it down
in seams and eddies
where a fish might be.

In the last light the deer come closer;
their long shadows give them courage.

I press my dog's forehead to my own
and hold it till I feel her calmness seep through,
till the restless equation I've made of the world
is simply the world again.

Bodhisattva

When the young man on State Street
approached as if to ask directions,
saying, "Can you help me out a little here?"
and I, though I already knew, said,
"Help you out how, exactly?"
"A dollar or two if you can,"
he said, and I took a deep breath,
holding in what I might've held out,
hearing *When someone asks, you
give what you can,* from my bank
of training in the ways of compassion,
and though I didn't want to,
opened my wallet, and
with the munificence of a toad,
pulled out a five and bought him off.

Doing Nothing

When I passed him near the bus stop
on Union Square while the cops
cuffed his hands behind his back, while he
said, "I didn't *do* anything,"
I didn't, either,
do anything but look away,
a little afraid they might cuff me
if I paid too much attention,
and walked on still wondering
what he might've done
and still more what I
might've done.

Realism

When he tells me how terribly he
misses his dead wife, I
diminish his grief by recounting my own.
I say this isn't tragic, it happens
to us all,
that *death* is the illusion, that time
will be unbroken, that a breeze
that doesn't happen to be blowing
is blowing.

Times Alone

Across the street from the theater
I stopped and looked into the restaurant,
saw a woman in a black dress laughing
at something another woman said,
wanted both women
and what made them laugh,
wanted to laugh too, for which,
I'd have given anything.

Fledgling

I see something looming in the road ahead.
Hulking might be a better word, though
what blocks the lane is no bigger than a possum.

A young redtail hawk,
her feathers still flocked with the cotton of childhood,
stripping the flesh from a flattened ground squirrel.

I drive a little closer and wait.

Her wings engulf her dead prize
as if to shelter it from the sun,
to keep it from the eyes of other birds,
and from me.

I pull around her and stop.

If my arm were three inches longer
I could touch her,
and still she holds her ground.

She lifts her head and glares at me.
This is my kill— Mine!
probably her first,
though she didn't kill it.

She is the eagle now,
and this *e pluribus unum,*
one of many
she will take to the sky.

Six Miles Up

The shadow of a hand brushes over the mountains,
as if smoothing rumpled sheets.
And now I see that the mountains are clouds.

In my dreams,
I search for what I won't remember in the morning,
but I do remember the searching.

In Venice I ate cuttlefish, steamed
in its own black ink,
and now it's coming out of my fingers.

Across the aisle in a window seat,
a man like me is
reading a book in which words appear,
tracing an indelible line
through invisible sky
while the pilot's skill keeps us flying.

A Small Dark Thing

A small dark thing darts across the room.
Or does it only dart across my eye?

The wake of a soul
probing toward the opposite shore?

We wonder who let the cat out when we
come home from work
to find her curled like smoke in the grass.

Someone who knows more than I'm willing to tell
calls late at night
when I'm just between dreams.

Out Walking in Early November

Only late sunlight
spattered under the oaks
and now a pair of redtails,
so effortlessly over the next range of hills
I wonder if they are taking it all in up there,
as I imagine,
and if they need me
to make it beautiful.

A Theory of Wind

for Django

The oxygen that the trees
conceive out of sunlight
backs up in the branches of a single oak.

A still morning, dead calm,
a new day just beginning
to penetrate the fog.

Maybe a crow calls to remind you
you are listening,
that the silence itself is a kind of song.

And then one tiny leaf starts to quiver.

The leaf, moved by your attention,
gives a little wave
and happens to brush another leaf,

and together they make a voice.

This glad commotion spreads along the limb
till the tree can't contain itself
any more than you can keep from hearing it
or feeling its breath on your face.

You are absolved of all responsibility now,
as the whole tree takes up this song,

which leaps like flame to the oak next door,

while the startled pine tries to hush it
and only makes matters worse
from the standpoint of stillness.

If you get down close to the ground now you will hear
how the normally complacent grass
is also infected.

You've seen it fan out in great swoops,
like a blush on the face of the sea.

In the Shade of the Oaks

Across the valley floor, the oaks are balls of consciousness,
absorbing small birds and the low-flying air.

Maybe they are no more conscious than their shadows,
but they envelop me in dreams
and their shadows, too.

In the evening I watch their shadows grow long,
like the hair of a man alone for a year,
while their limbs grow dense
to the song their cells sing,
round after round.

Can you say "pertinacious"? Can you
say it ten times and still make sense?

Will you lie down here in the shade of these oaks?
Will you let your shadow lie down?

Getting It Right, or Wrong

In a poem called
"Portrait of the Artist as a Young Boy,"
Joseph Stroud wrote:
"The boy is making something
for the girl he has a crush on,"
which I read, "*of* the girl he has a crush on,"
not making of her flesh — not
that kind of poem —
but a memory of the
warm way she smelled
when he stood close behind her
in the gym and the blush he felt
his nearness may have caused.

He paints, in that dreaming, half-life
part of his brain, moonlight
streaming through a tall window,
sheer curtains drifting
in from the casements, a
diaphanous gown
floating around her,
in which he's floating, too,
angel voices serenading and then
seeming to condemn
the throbbing intention he's smuggled
into this dream.

Autumn on the Plains of Idaho

The air is a god, and the water
is a god;
we move through them, and they
move through us. *For the kingdom*
is within you and without you.
And snow weaves through the heads of the sage.

There Is No Self That Suffers Rebirth

Kenneth Rexroth

After an all-night rain,
it's Tuesday.
Leaf shadows dazzle the west wall of my room,
and clouds still nuzzle the soaked grass
in a few deep cuts
across the valley. Doves scatter
in a sudden breeze
and the branches of the oak
out my window
rustle this morning's absolution
to the girl in the stonewashed sky.

Madam Wei Remembers

aka Wei Wan ca. 1050

How we both looked down
to where you disappeared inside me.
I lifted my head from the pillow to watch
that mysterious dark child come between us.

Once in Nineveh

I paused on a hillside, eavesdropping
on a quiet conversation between two neighboring oaks
in a light afternoon breeze,
the throbbing of a small Cessna,
the ground-tone roar of a jet
at a much greater distance, and one
persistent crow, cawing the same note
over and over, as if believing the world
too obtuse to acknowledge his existence,
or that it may be, as he is now,
simply not listening.

Candor Seeks Its Own Unforeseeable Occasions

Hayden Carruth

Tonight the sky is holding its breath.
A dove moans in the rain.
The moon is a thousand miles wide.
Maybe I'll get lucky and take the wrong road.

The Call

My dog watches me with unblinking eyes,
a look she can hold forever, it seems.
She wants me to know what she knows —
that the law of the universe demands it —
that behind her steady gaze
open all the fields we've longed to cover,
thickets waiting to snag our coats,
ticks poised to drop from the trees,
coyote turds we must piss on,
that the earth is deep with unknowable others
and the odors they've left to entice us —
    if only I could smell them —
might be the actual handkerchief *designedly dropped*
by that dark daughter of memory
I've been courting all morning.

Revenant

When I looked up again
I could see the fox from my window,
watching as she would every day
on my walk,
from her cover of mullein and snakeweed,
barking her curt, raucous bark
till I scanned the hillside
and our eyes met,
                    as if, by some pact,
made back in the primordial when our
trails first crossed,
we had agreed on this still,
shrouded morning in June
to question these two
of our ten thousand lives.

Late Summer

Two mongrels, one mostly shepherd, one chow,
wandered up each day from the canyon
while we worked on the barn.
They didn't seem to be hungry,
asked nothing from us,
and slept all day in the shade of the walls
on the cool loam
of the not-yet-fenced-in corral.

They lived somewhere to the north
was all we knew, or assumed,
since the canyon was north,
and they, for their part, assumed nothing,
only that our land was theirs to warm with their bellies
and that we were welcome to it
while we nailed the roof beams in place.

Just before Sunset

We paused at our ranch gate and looked past the hayfield
at shadows on the mesa.

The air was still hot at quarter to nine,
though we dipped through cool eddies
on our walk from the barn.

Second cutting, and the cab of the reaper
loomed over its blades like the bridge of a tug.

It wheeled at the end of the row,
plowing its way back over bow waves of dust
as it churned through the still, green hay.

The Changes in Santa Ynez

Through the last long weeks of summer
I waited for fall,
    though you'd hardly know it,
so subtle here,
a tinge in the vineyards,
stately old tarantula crossing the road
on his way to die for love.

Now it's come, and I'm hardly aware,
a paler blue in the sky,
the blanket I pull up
from the foot of the bed at three a.m.,
the familiar books of longing I turn to,
the rustle of leaves I've walked through before.

TWO

We linger in manhood to tell the dreams of our childhood,
and they are half forgotten ere we have learned the language.

THOREAU

Eclipse

Our shadow sweeps the Sea of Tranquillity
till we're only a small bruise on the moon's left temple.

Fears of Childhood

In you, who were a child once — in you.

RILKE

From the bedroom window,
across my father's garden,
beyond the high picket fence,
a single light from city hall
casts a shadow of branches,
like crickets praying
on the wall above my head.

The night is humming somewhere in that darkness
where men in black clothes
are preparing a death for my mother,
dragging her down a long corridor
through pools of overhead light,
far ahead, weeping.
I hear my own screams in her voice,
silent in the dark, then loud in the light,
a fatal Morse code, till she leaves me
alone in the adamant night.

❧

She came to me as a stranger,
stumbling from the din of music
and voices down the hall,
slipped under the covers, weeping,
and held me with her terrors,
smelling of the night, of heaviness,

of unfamiliar hands and a slurred lullaby.
I held her away with stiffened arms,
till finally, when the door was closed again,
a light along the threshold refrained,
Someday you won't have me. Someday
you'll be sorry...

♦

Still she was my mother,
still a child,
so full of longing for the world she knew,
and nothing she knew I didn't feel
moving through me as a shadow.

Momma's Boy

How many times she kept him out of school
to see *Gone with the Wind,* he couldn't tell,
only that she wept
when Scarlett lost Ashley Wilkes, again and again,
and was quiet after,
and drove to the lake and sang lullabies
and held his body to her awkwardly
until he sensed
something more than a movie was at stake.

And then she took him home and left him
with the nursemaid of the hour
and drove away for days to see her sick friend,
Betty, she would say. Betty was always sick
it seemed, her function to be there —
wherever *there* may be — and to need
his mother's care.

When his father called from Cleveland
or New York, he told him Mommy was away,
that Betty was sick again and needed her,
as he'd been told to say. Though once,
when he was supposed to be asleep,
the phone rang and he picked it up
to hear his mother saying to a man
how she could hardly wait and
in two days' time would be there,
and told him in the morning

how Betty had fallen
and broken her hip and she'd be taking him
to stay with Joppi on the farm
until she could come home again,
and then, that in a year or so, she'd be
sending him away to school
where they would make a man of him.

He watched her car become a dust-plume
and turn the corner north and fade
up over North Stone Road, and then
the crickets sang to him, and Joppi
called him in to supper.

One Sunday Night

The principal of his grade school
hung himself from a rafter,
and he didn't remember now,
or ever know why.

It was his first encounter with
the idea that a man or a woman may decide
not to be here anymore, and actually accomplish
the feat his mother had tried so many times,
playing above the net of discovery.

                                  To his father,
it was a powerful argument that she
should have whatever it may be, at the moment
she washed down yellow pills
with good Scotch, and a few blue ones
thrown in for aesthetic relief.

WWII

His mother blowing smoke rings in his ear
to soothe the earaches that came back
so she would hold him in her arms
another night and smoke another Lucky Strike
and sing another lullaby or tell another story
of how nothing was either wrong or right
but thinking made it so, that the earaches kept coming back
because the bad thoughts wanted out and he was
hoarding them inside, stubborn like his father,
"And your grandfather, too," she added,
the way you toss things unintended
on the fire you built
to burn up what you didn't want.

Meanwhile the war news on the radio,
something about Saipan—one of those words
like Tarawa or later Bastogne that conjured
ruined trees in black and white—a palm
with only two fronds left or half a plane tree
like a signpost, pointing a way the highway didn't go,
accompanied by the breezy music of longing, *not
sitting under the apple tree or being home for Christmas,*
though not this year—and looking back, home
seemed a place he'd never really been because
now it was a place he couldn't go, longing for longing,
for what he saw finally as old sorrows
in the amber light of memory, but longing still
because it filled the cold and terrifying space he called
the present, and all the gaping presents
waiting to become.

Christmas Eve 1944

He remembered his mother singing
"Silent Night" in German
and how odd it seemed, now
we were bombing the people
who sang in that tongue.

And just down the road, in a maze of barbed wire,
under the watchful eye of a gun,
soldiers who would sing *"Stille Nacht"*
were being kept in the snow,
waiting for the war to be over.

In the hall outside his bedroom,
a painting one of the men had done for his mother,
who supplied him with canvas
and all the colors he remembered
of his home in the snow that was falling there, too,
and where,
if the bombs weren't at that moment also falling,
or even more likely if they were,
his wife and two daughters might still be singing
"Stille Nacht,"
through what seemed to him, now,
the not so quiet night.

The Rain Poured Down

My mother weeping
in the dark hallway, in the arms of a man,
not my father,
as I sat at the top of the stairs unnoticed—
my mother weeping and pleading
for what I didn't know and can still only imagine—
for things to be somehow other than they were,
not knowing what I would change,
for, or to, or why,
only that my mother was weeping
in the arms of a man not me,
and the rain brought down the winter sky
and hid me in the walls that looked on,
indifferent to my mother's weeping,
or mine,
in the rain that brought down the dark afternoon.

Then

When I was seven, or maybe eight, I rode with my mother out to a farm where something I was told we wouldn't speak of had happened. A man and a woman, young, as I remember—though all adults were old to me then—met her in the yard of that unpainted house and received the gift of food she brought, a casserole with tuna, and bread she had baked to a golden, nutty brown. I remember that I was made to stay in the back of our black '47 Chevrolet, and remember all this because of a worm on the mohair carpet, a worm squashed and glistening on the floor, and that the hair of the perhaps young woman was curly, as if it had lately been in ringlets, and that her face was so pale and haunted that I loved her, loved at least the sadness of her life, and that the woman and the man—who had black hair, I remember—stood in the yard and watched as my mother backed the car in the dry autumn grass and said to me over her shoulder, with a look not unlike that of the woman who was watching, "Remember this, and how lucky you are," though I don't remember why, only the feeling, the wonder left—the rest lost to childhood— and the sad young woman, so pale I could smell her, like sleep or the must of old lilacs, still waving after the man turned away, and the unlucky worm, green and still glistening, as the shadows of trees swept the floor and the Chevrolet whined away through its gears.

BOOK LOFT
1680 MISSION DRIVE
SOLVANG, CA 93463
805-688-6010
MAIL@BOOKLOFTSOLVANG.COM

24-Apr-08   7:07 PM
Clerk: Admin Register # 3

Trans. #10048635
   * - Non Taxable Items

CHASE, DIANA

 Customer ID: 6882862

9781556592539   1 $15.00 $15.00
   PRIMER ON PARALLEL LIVE
Total Items: 1
                Sub-Total: $15.00
             Tax @ 7.750%: $1.16
                   Total: $16.16
           Total Tendered: $16.16
              Change Due: $0.00

Payment Via:
    VISA/MC/Discover $6.16
    Coupon $10.00

BOOK LOFT
1680 MISSION DRIVE
SOLVANG, CA 93463
805-688-6010
MAILGREENLOFTSOLVANG.COM

24-Nov-08   1:07 PM
Clerk: Robin Register # 3

Trans. #1004635
* - Non Taxable Items

CHASE, DIANO

Customer ID: 6882802

9781556592539   1 $15.00 $15.00
PRIMER OF PARALLEL LIVE
Total Items: 1

Sub-Total: $15.00
Tax @ 7.7500: $1.16
Total: $16.16
Total Tendered: $16.16
Change Due: $0.00

Payment Via:
VISA/MC/Discover $6.16
Coupon $10.00

Mountaineer—Third Grade

The truck turned the corner, and Lynn ran up
the bank of snow piled high as a mountain
to climb and then, pretending,
fall back from,
sliding down a crevasse or couloir,
some famous climber's death I'd gathered
from a book of expeditions in the Alps,
a garden mattock for a climbing tool
and clothesline round our army-surplus coats,
to hold the fallen and pull them back.
But then there was the truck,
a Reo semi-rig,
rumbling down the glacier of our snow-packed street—
nothing before, ever quite so final—
poor Lynn sliding—
nothing again, ever quite so sure.

On Being Sent Away to School

When they called me to the office to tell me my grandfather was dead, when Herbie Schellenberger, ex-corporal of the Third Reich, who seemed old to a classroom of twelve-year-old boys and told us, with ill-suppressed laughter, how funny things were in the war, how his lieutenant, having failed in his duty at Bastogne, put the water-filled barrel of a Luger in his mouth and how silly he looked with his head reduced to the size of saucepan, ridiculed the sentimentality of my missing so much Latin because an old man was dead, how that first poem, "The Highwayman" by Alfred Noyes, was my ticket to a light less harsh where a beautiful woman gave her life for love, and how a mist I might not have otherwise seen rose from the frost on the grass as the sun beat down through the late autumn morning while I lugged my suitcase out to catch the bus that would take me on that long ride back to where a month ago I was a child.

The Day I Fled My Twelve-year-old Life

A river broadly flowing:
I crossed to an island in a rented boat—
green oars, green boat, green
kingdom where I found,
for that one day, and years beyond,
another boy who could be me.

He had an easier way about him,
not smarting from the sting of school,
not lonely, though he lived alone,
not pining for his mother far away.
He rustled in the trees all afternoon
and purled in the current as it
hugged the island and moved on.

His spirits were snakes and birds and frogs.
His voice was in the breeze.
He told me I could come again,
that he'd be there, or anywhere,
if I would be there, too. If I
would just remember him,
the river, the boat, the bees,
and how the water
dazzled-back the sunlight
through the trees.

Her Eyes

He learned his longing from his mother.
Her eyes reached out for what she couldn't see
and framed a space he'd have to fill
with other eyes that never rested,
and never could it seemed.

Later he'd see them in an airport,
or waiting for a train,
unaware how sad
the light in which he saw them made them seem,
or how her forlorn smile infected him —
his need to be just what she needed,
though she'd never know his name,
or why he looked at her, or how,
     if she were filled with him,
she wouldn't look that way.

Photograph of My Father

His dark eyes look right out,
as if to say, *I'm here.*
His sergeant's stripes almost disguised
by the coarse cloth of his tunic,
and I wonder if this photo came before
or after he came back from Château-Thierry,
and those nightmare thickets in Argonne.

From the fullness of his lips, about to smile,
you couldn't tell;
that same near-smile I saw,
sixty years later,
begin to cross his face before he died,
a smile to say, *I get it now*
and know.

A Star at Dawn, a Bubble in a Stream

And what if it's true,
as my mother insisted in her final years,
that she'd never married, never given birth,
that the memory of my childhood is a story I was told,
or concocted from old books and movies,
that I may be the product of someone else's dream,
set free like the second stage of a rocket,
to dream and imagine even more?

But then there are all the old photographs
and a birth certificate, though I've never seen it,
the recounting of my twelve-pound delivery,
my first spanking at sixth months
when I stiffened out in my high chair,
the legend of my learning to walk,
grasping the fur of my Great Pyrenees dog,
my first historical memory, the day the war ended
in August, two days after I turned five,
my first day of kindergarten and six more
decades I've spun out
to convince you, imagined reader,
busy as you must be
with your own anthropic freight.

The Man Jumping

My mother's thumb is rubbed raw on the end, the nail broken.
Something is wrong, but she can't tell me what it is or maybe
she doesn't know. Her thoughts trail away in half sentences,
It... I need... Could you... Maybe... I tug her back up the
plane of the bed when her shoulder slips under the rail, but she
slumps down again like a cushion with the stiffness gone out of
it. I straighten her pillows. Her eyes dart over the wall, as if a
dozen visitors were milling in the room. *Why is that man
jumping?* she asks, her eyes wide with surprise, and I sit by the
bed, hoping she might say something I'll understand, that maybe
she'll answer my question. Why is her thumb torn? She looks at
it now and flicks it with her finger. "Your thumb's all raw,
Mother," I say, the dead skin shredded as if flayed on rough
stone. *Why is he jumping?* She looks at me through her
quavering eyes, and I sit still wondering about the woman I
knew, wondering why the man is jumping and
who he might be.

The Distance Between Us

On this ill-formed winter afternoon, my mother
sits holding herself at the edge of her bed,
as if to comfort some disembodied other.

Fog rises from the snow below her window,
and the trees stand out like dead lightning
across a coagulated sky.

She rolls her eyes in my direction
and whines in a child's tiny voice,
"I want to go home. They don't feed me here."

This is your home, I try to tell her.
I point to the family photos on the table,
but the woman who might've seen them isn't here
and hasn't been for a decade,
as the disease between us spins the calendar back,
till I'm now simply a strange, familiar man
who often comes to see her.

"I could be nice to you,"
she greets me in her *come-hither* lilt,
with a shrug of her eyebrows,
each day as I enter her room.

But now she's four years old again,
pining for a home I can't provide.

"I can't find my parents," she cries.
I pull my chair up close to her bed
and cradle her hands in mine.
"Where do you think they might be?"
I ask.

"I don't know," she whimpers.
Then everything changes —
"I'd like to *cook* 'em," she growls,
her face now beaming with absolute glee.

Sail Baby Sail

Now I sing to my mother, the lullabies she sang to me as a child. Her hand trembles to her mouth, as if to find the lips that once formed words, as if to move them again with her fingers into speech. She makes a face at me, and bounces her eyebrows as she would when she sang, *Gunk, gunk went the little bull froggy,* and I smooth back her hair as I sing to her now, *Gunk, gunk went the lady froggy, too.* She laughs, and for a moment her trembling is gone. She holds her smile like a note sustained at the end of a phrase, like a child waiting for another surprise. I tickle her forehead, and remember a twilight over her shoulder, or think I remember, and the creaking of the chair as we rocked and the perfume she wore. *Sail baby sail,* I half mumble, half sing, *far across the sea. Only don't forget to sail, home again to me.* She cries, and I catch her tear in a tissue, my "tear catcher," I call it, and she laughs. Something is passing between us, something I felt a dozen years ago as I talked to my father long after he'd stopped breathing, something that holds us together, something like music, something we might carry to another life, like the sound of a human voice talking.

Dorothy

How can that depth be fathomed where a man may see himself reflected?

THOREAU

I held her hand through her last drugged sleep
and called the names that used to make her smile
    Mother, Mom,
names I'd pled with as a child
to let me be with her.

Dorothy Marion Scott, she insisted
as her illness worked its course,
never married, never gave birth,
still asking for her parents,
as if they'd suddenly been called away
or simply wandered off
to view some paintings in a church
far away.

My words were only sounds now, coming back.
just slight rhyme and assonance,
until I said, "Dorothy,"
the name I'd never called before.

Her eyes opened.
I saw myself there twice.
I wonder who she was just then,
and if she saw me gazing in
before they closed again.

Lying under the Oaks on a Morning in June

I can't tell now if I'm drifting
among the branches or the roots,
rising into the clear spring sky
or drawn down to lie
with those dear, departed selves
I loved and couldn't help
but go on loving.

THREE

Stag's Head: Albrecht Dürer, 1504

The arrow has gone deep,
almost to the feathers,
impaling the delicate brain
through the flat ridge of bone
to the right of the stag's left eye,
which is open
and still just moist enough
to reflect the light by which it was painted,
though the head has been severed,
and the liver may already have been eaten.

Ancient ancestor
of the three young doe
who came to my window this morning
to browse on my rosemary and lavender.

The eye looks up and out
with the beleaguered air
of a mild injustice,
the wound itself a protuberant labia
gripping the arrow's shaft, and the
fine, stiff hairs below the eye
have the stippled texture of old walnut,
through which a worm has been wearing
a trough toward the nose. Lament,
the poet said,
is the progenitor of praise.
The murdered head of Orpheus
kept on singing.

My Life with the Muse

She says *sky wheel* meaning *windmill.*
By what sweet mystery are we drawn together?

"To simply say 'I love you' is sappy," she says.
"Do I have to invent my own dreams?"

I field her complaints
by letting them pass.

They are her way of knowing herself,
and she knows it.

"I loved my food," my father said
at the very end of his life.

"I love my fuel," says the engine
that sings so sweetly through its gears.

"Are we only the conjecture we take for our lives?"
"Yes," she says, "but not only.

"And not conjecture exactly,
in this world we imagine by calling it real."

Sometimes

I fall in love with that one
glimpse of her from behind,
something about the bend of her arm,
the tilt of her head now, listening,
or simply the weight and sheen of her hair,
hoping sooner or later she may turn,
that she might be someone I loved once,
or the other me I sense now
standing beside me may have loved.

Six Kinds of Gratitude

1

I'm someone's small boat,
far out at sea,
sailing from what has so long sustained me
toward what I don't know.

My joy is the sound
of the water purling around me,
but is it my hull
or the great ocean moving?

2

Are those flies I hear, or a trick of the wind,
faintly human voices,
or a whistle of breath
in the nose of my sleeping dog?

3

Without *me* there is no confusion.
Buddhas see no difference between
themselves and others; Angels,
between the living and the dead.

4

At last I've discovered
the secret of life:
If you don't leave
you can't come back.

5

Deep in the Earth there are pockets of light
that did not come from Heaven,
and yet they are the light of Heaven
deep inside the Earth.

6

This bird is the birdness of a bird.

Facing North

Ninety billion galaxies in this one tiny universe—
a billion seconds make thirty-two years.

No matter how many ways we conceive it,
this generous wedge called Ursa Major
more than fills my sight.

But now, as I turn to put out the lights
and give my dog her bedtime cookie,
my eyes become the handle of the great Milky Way,
and carry it into the house.

Five Poems: Off the Beaten Track

1

Deep in the mountains;
few friends come to see us.

At times we experience the past as an avalanche,
at others as an anchor,
till our raft is swept
beyond the sight of land
on water we haven't yet seen.

2

My dog barks,
announcing the arrival of Tuesday.

She watches it lumber through the oaks
after creeping up the hill from the sea.

Life is always three or four things
occurring to me all at one time.

3

I want to preserve this dawn —
a small stone we can suck on.

Everything flies away, and a photograph
is only a photograph, especially
of something so beautiful.

4

Without even trying
this white pebble radiates
tiny white rings with a vitreous humor,

a moon leaving Saturn
in the nick of time.

5

White cattle wend their way
along the canyon road.

Saints in procession under the oaks.

The Oaks in the Fog

The oaks aren't only for my delight.
But then again, maybe they are.
Edging my way in the morning fog,
I take it on faith they are here at all,
that they haven't slipped away to where oak trees go
when they weary of taking on our feelings.

Forms, perceptions, consciousness,
no more mine than theirs.
I walk toward where I think I last saw them,
a thickening of the air and then, a tree.
I have sent for you in the names of the Father—
their great black arms reaching into the morning,
happy at last I am here.

The Local News

For sixty-four years now
my heart has worked without praise,
without benefits, time off, or even a
certificate of appreciation.
It stumbles only when it comes across beauty,
    previewing the loss of something it loves,
or with the loss itself, which finally comes down to
looking at beauty across a divide,
unattainable but for the moment that keeps
it, and the moment, alive.

I've always been one of those who look back—
    half Zennist, half Goddist, my Zen master said—
like Orpheus. Or Lot's wife, whom I know
I'd have coveted,
given my intrinsic predilection for salt.

I think of her as *Margot,* though
the concocters of Genesis
never bothered to give her a name,
and given the chance I know I'd go back for her,
as I know I would for Eurydice, too,
disregarding, for a moment,
the fickle nature of memory
and who I might be when her hand touches mine.

Domestic

For you, it's how they look;
for me, it's how they feel—
in this case, the cushions on the sofa.

Fashion is the mother of death,
someone wisely said.

What speaks *life* to this moment
speaks *death* to the next.

Those narrow lapels will come back again,
you say.

Mornings after a Marriage

He wakes as if from a bad dream
to discover the bad dream of waking,
a grieving that could only bring
more grief—that the warmth we desire
also burns us.

Secrets

Sometimes I see the shadow of a bird
cross my path
and can't find a bird in the sky.

The dolphin sleeps with only half her brain.
She must surface to breathe or she'll die.

Wild pigs have been rooting up
under the oaks again.
Last summer they tore the whole yard—
not an inch of grass left facing the sky.

The vulture claps her wings and
goose-steps under the tree.

*The cistern contains: the fountain
overflows.*

The lord of desire wants the cup to be empty.

Grass Mountain

My old dog's eyes stay with me,
though she's gone,
and take my eyes now, seeing in
to what is looking out, not longing,
but how to see the thing inside itself,
the sky in sky, the grass in grass,
but not just grass and sky.

A thousand years ago or so
we came to a hilltop
and paused to catch our breath, like lovers,
unaware of being two,
or even one.

I pause there now again.

The yarrow smells like sage.

We are what wants to be.

Dear Reader

A metaphor is a species of symbol. So is a lover.
ANNE CARSON

In my dream I am a woman
lying on my bed in a diaphanous dress,
open to the world and the night.

I woke up with a hard-on,
a little afraid —
perhaps desiring the woman I was,
as Aristophanes perceived the symbol of our lives,
a search for the missing half?

In my dream I wonder
if I am you —
and the dream itself, a glimpse beyond
the frontier of that promised country,
partitioned by a lord called I.

The Sonnets to Orpheus

Half my life I've pursued them,
insistent as lichen eating into stone,
determined to understand their Attic terrain
through the mist of my expectations,

as if, with enough concerted looking,
I could will the hills to appear.
But while I was straining to see them,
the hills were rising inside me.

When they sing of rain, I'm a desert;
when they change to sun, I become a willing tree,
my leaves transforming the light of their words
into what I already am, un-
til there is no outside world anymore.

Watching the Leopard at the Chester Zoo

She stops in midstride and locks her eyes on mine,
then steals on toward me,
as if my gaze were a door left open
to a world she still believes in,
and creeps closer still
till our eyes are all the world there is.

She stalks me this way seven more times,
turning at the opposite wall,
then circles herself and curls and sleeps,

and I let myself go in her dream,
a forest without partitions or signs,
through which the warm, pale light
of her animal eyes
leads us on.

Eagle on His Own

I spot a young eagle on a lower branch
upslope from the river,
through a break in gnarled pine,
spreading his great coverts and folding them again,
and again, as if rehearsing his eagleness.

Maybe he's only drying his feathers,
or stretching his tendons for some pure joy
of stretching,
but right now I prefer to imagine him,
the self-anointed sovereign of his *wild surmise,*
directing the river's flow as he pleases,
scalloping its riffles with his long-fingered will,
unabashedly showing off
for the curious fisherman on the bank below,
imagining him soaring in his own mind, too.

2004

When your country has been a bad citizen again
and you're a little ashamed of her,
as you were of your four-year-old
when she threw another tantrum at the mall,
and you wanted to pretend you didn't know her,
that you weren't responsible for her bad behavior,
a citizen of the world, as you wish she would be.

Still her mountains glow in the late evening sun,
and your neighbors, who voted to support her arrogance,
smile kindly when you greet them, and you're moved,
observing their obvious affection for each other,
how he pulls up her collar against the chill breeze
and she smooths back his comb-over again and again.

You saw this in Cincinnati and again in Darfur,
people being conscious and considerate of others,
and you wonder how we ever draw the line
about whom we choose to comfort and whom
it might be quite permissible to kill.

Heroes

*The Grail is being in perfect accord with the abundance
of nature.*

JOSEPH CAMPBELL

The path Buddha took away from the world
was the path he took coming back,
but when Ulysses returned home from Troy
he came a much longer way.

Falling into habits you become a target;
whoever wants to may do you great harm,
though being a target may be who you are.

Suppose Jesus kissed Judas and snuck out of the garden,
or the Buddha returned to his palace as a beggar
and slew all the louts who took up with his wife,
or Ulysses sailed back in sunlight,
a gentle old man now, anointed in blood,
and forgave those who trespassed against him,

or that Parzival found the abiding Grail—
that question killed by an answer—
and sold it.

A Primer on Parallel Lives

Bees and sprinklers employ the silence,
and a horse screaming over the hill.

According to Euclid, Hades has no depth,
no echoes, no valleys, no heart's embrace.

Now the faintest curve of a sycamore
begins to shine through the fog,

and the window we look out of
becomes the frame in which we're displayed.

When I Have Doubts

Jesus says that if the Kingdom
is up in the air,
the birds will be there before you,
and if in the sea, the fishes
will have it as their own.

But tell me, dear Jesus,
isn't that just, and just
as it should be?

At Any Moment

This anger sneaks back in
like the thought of a white horse
I'm determined to ignore,
my heart on fire with intolerance
of intolerance,
the wars I fight against the wars
in me. I have come to regret
being right about anything.

Contemplating My Reflection in a Puddle on the Last Day of the Twentieth Century

Even this still water wants to be somewhere else,
another way of saying it's motion
seeking space,
drawn to the earth as rain,
or into the air as vapor,
off on a quest, in-
eluctably drawn to find itself,
disguised in you and me.

A Walk in the Clouds

Day after day
I waited for a phone call
that would change my life, a letter
from someone not of this world —
for a sure sign to tell me
what I already know.

On the lime tree in my garden
some of the branches are heavy with fruit,
while others are just beginning to blossom.

When I got back to my house
someone was waiting,
shoes soaked with dew, clothes
silver with fog,
face faint and fading
in my breath on the mirror.

One Last Wish

Which of the gods will dare thy judge to be?
BAUDELAIRE

When you read this after I've gone
it will seem like an old story,
my constellation of quirks,
a memory, still no less
than I ever was.

The thing about a movie, no matter
how many times through,
you harbor small hopes that
this once the letter will arrive in time,
the heart soften and forgive, the ache
soothed before the credits roll.

To Study the Way

My world this morning made simple
by the fog out my window,
this one tree, and beyond it
no distant mountains
through the large, open windows of the oak,
no pale grass hillside, or horses,
no deer standing stark still, listening
for any movement, looking
back my way for some slight
sign I may be watching,
whoever I may be.

After the Rain

I spot a young barn owl
standing by the road
peering at his own reflection in a puddle,
or so it seems,
when I pull off on the shoulder to see
if I can help.

Dazed,
probably struck by a car,
though not visibly wounded,
he looks up across the puddle
where I'm standing,
as if to ask about this
wondrous, underground bird he is seeing,
as if to ask if I see it, too.

Some Distance

I wanted to be a stone in the field,
simply that,
and then I wanted to be the grass around it,
and then the cattle grazing
under the too blue sky,
and then the blue,
which has of itself
no substance,
and yet goes on and on and on.

About the Author

Dan Gerber has published six previous collections of poetry, three novels, a book of short stories, and two books of nonfiction. His *Trying to Catch the Horses* received *ForeWord* magazine's Gold Medal Book of the Year Award in Poetry. Gerber's work has appeared in *The New Yorker, Poetry, The Georgia Review,* and *Best American Poetry.* With his wife, Debbie, and with numerous animals, he lives in the Santa Ynez Valley of central California.

The Chinese character for poetry is made up of two parts: "word" and "temple." It also serves as pressmark for Copper Canyon Press.

Since 1972, Copper Canyon Press has fostered the work of emerging, established, and world-renowned poets for an expanding audience. The Press thrives with the generous patronage of readers, writers, booksellers, librarians, teachers, students, and funders—everyone who shares the belief that poetry is vital to language and living.

Major funding has been provided by:

Anonymous (2)

The Paul G. Allen Family Foundation

Lannan Foundation

National Endowment for the Arts

Washington State Arts Commission

THE **PAUL G. ALLEN**
FAMILY *foundation*

NATIONAL
ENDOWMENT
FOR THE ARTS

WASHINGTON
STATE ARTS
COMMISSION

For information and catalogs:

COPPER CANYON PRESS
Post Office Box 271
Port Townsend, Washington 98368
360-385-4925
www.coppercanyonpress.org

This book is set in Adobe Garamond, a revival of type from the early 1500s by Claude Garamond. Type designer Robert Slimbach created the digital form you see here. The book title is set in Monotype Garamond, based on the work of Jean Jannon. Jannon's work from the early 1600s was long misidentified and is the basis of many revivals bearing the name "Garamond." Book design and composition by Valerie Brewster, Scribe Typography. Printed on archival-quality Glatfelter Author's Text by McNaughton & Gunn, Inc.